The 21 Financial Myths

ENJOY!

Dan Wyson, CFP®

ISBN 978-0-9771522-0-9

PREFACE

While boarding a commuter flight to Los Angeles I watched the pilot inspect the plane as he always did. He carefully turned the propellers on the old turbo-prop, carefully looking at each one. I had seen pilots do this on every flight, even though they flew back and forth five or six times a day.

I turned and asked the pilot what he was looking for and why the constant inspection. He replied to me, "A very small crack becomes a very large problem at 25,000 feet."

That answer was sufficient for me and I realized my business was not all that different. I am in the business of helping people get to their destination; a destination which may be 20 or 30 years or more down the road.

I make a point to always proceed with the destination in mind, realizing, as this pilot did, that a very small crack in today's financial vehicle can grow into a very big problem many years down the road.

The purpose of this book is not to solve your financial problems. As I am not an attorney, nor a CPA, it is not designed to give legal or tax advice. Investors should consult their tax or legal professional for specific advice on these matters.

Its purpose is not to advise you on how to proceed with your investing. I am not attempting to recommend investments, strategies or plans. I am merely one small pilot showing you a few ways to inspect your financial propellers to see if there are any cracks.

TABLE OF CONTENTS

A DIFFICULT DECISION

It all started with doughnuts. It isn't often that a book on financial *anything* begins with doughnuts, but this one does. It begins with doughnuts because after 41 years I can still smell them as if they were freshly baked this morning.

They say that smell evokes the most powerful memory of all the senses and I must agree with whoever *they* are. Every Monday the yellow bread truck would pull into our driveway and honk his familiar horn. I would immediately drop whatever serious project I was involved in at the young age of five, and run to get to the back door of the truck before the driver could open it up. It was important that I be standing in just the right place or else I would miss what was about to happen.

As he swung those huge doors wide open, a world of a five year olds dreams was revealed in all its splendor. Row upon row of dark wooden drawers, each with a glass front so you could see the delicious pastries inside, lay before my eyes beckoning me like a bunch of anxious children yelling "pick me, pick me." More beautiful however than the sight was indescribable smell of breads, cookies, pies and doughnuts that flooded out and sent me into near childhood ecstasy.

As I stood there soaking up the wonder of it all, my mom would arrive and claim her weekly order of fresh bread - five loaves of wheat and one rye. It rarely changed. For this I was grateful because that meant she would always receive the same nickel as change. Glancing at the nickel as if she was trying to decide what to do with it, though I knew better, she would then smile and say "Danny, do you want to buy a doughnut today?" She asked it like it was a decision to be made. The only decision for me was what kind my mouth was currently watering for.

The above event repeated itself for the better part of six months, until one day it all changed. I had followed the script perfectly, running to the back of the truck, watching the driver sling open the doors, getting ready to take that first big smell, when suddenly something caught my eye from behind a drawer on the left side. Right there, staring out at me in all its glory was the most coveted item the world had to offer. It was that one thing no single five year old on the planet could do without--a 45 rpm record containing the theme song to Astro Boy. As an avid TV watcher at the time, I considered myself one of the biggest Astro Boy fans of all time. I excitedly asked the bread man about the record and he told me his company was selling them until they ran out for twenty-five cents. I almost tackled my mother when she arrived as I begged and begged for one of those records.

Unfortunately my mom saw this as one of those unpleasant learning experiences. Kids hate it when parents do that. She told me that if I would do jobs for her during the week she would pay me enough money to buy the record. I was certain she had misjudged the high demand on the records and was certain that there was no way there would be any left the following week when the bread truck returned. Still, there was no moving her so I watched in sorrow as the yellow truck pulled away with my Astro Boy record locked inside.

During the next week I spent time each day doing a chore for my mom, and in return she would give me a nickel. She had explained to me that it would take five of them to buy the record. Even though I was sure the records would be all gone, I continued working on the slight hope that there might be just one left. After what seemed like a thousand weeks, I was one day sitting in the living room when I heard the honk of that wonderful yellow bread truck. I ran to the back door of the truck and waited, it seemed hours, for the driver to get out and open it up. I wasn't thinking about the smell this time. I had only one goal. Quickly I searched the upper shelves and my eyes nearly popped out of my head when I saw there were still some left.

"I want Astro Boy, I want Astro Boy" I frantically said to the driver.

With a smile he lifted one off the shelf for me as he said, "that will be twenty-five cents."

I held out my hand to give him my five nickels and just as he was about to take them a powerful realization fell upon me. I pulled my hand back to gaze at the nickels. Never before had they looked the same. I always considered it strange that the bread man would trade me a delicious creamy doughnut for a little round piece of metal. Now, as I gazed down at those nickels I no longer saw little pieces of metal. I saw five delicious doughnuts. Standing at the back of that bread truck at the age of five I was being given my first lesson in finance. I was not trading nickels for a record, I was trading five wonderful doughnuts. After some pause, I made the purchase, but now I viewed Astro Boy through more intelligent eyes, and with a much greater appreciation for what he had cost me.

Birth of a Philosophy

It would be nice to think it was Astro Boy from whom I learned my lessons about the real value of money, but unfortunately, like most, I learned my lessons slowly and with some difficulty in the beginning.

I began investing in various markets back in the early 80's. You will remember Jimmy Carter was president, the Prime rate topped out at 21% and inflation was threatening to hit double digits. In the midst of this national crisis, I saw opportunity. Of course back then I was much younger, and not as wise as I thought I was.

It was about that time that the Famous Hunt brothers set out on a campaign to corner the silver market. They were rich and successful and surely knew what they were doing, so I decided the easy road to wealth would be to ride their coattails. I began buying silver knowing that it would soon top $100 and ounce and I would be rich.

Before my 23rd birthday I had succeeded in losing $10,000 chasing silver – chasing it downward. That was enough money in those days to buy a really nice new car. Memories of Astro Boy returned, only now I was weighing a new car against some worthless silver futures. I decided there had to be a better way.

My first job, if you can call it that, in the financial world was working as a go-fer for a Gold Mining Investment Firm in Las Vegas. My job was to go out and meet with people who had expressed an interest in investing in mining shares and gather information from them. If they seemed to be legitimate prospects I would turn them over to the senior sales people.

It didn't take long before I noticed a distinct pattern forming in my meetings with these people. An experience with a man I shall name Saul is typical of many others.

Saul was a wealthy owner of large chain of convenience stores in Las Vegas. He was respected in the community and known for his sharp business senses. When I walked into Saul's office I looked around at the expensive furniture and souvenirs from his world travels, and quickly realized I was out of my league.

Still, I had a job to do. I was too young to know how to make small talk with such a giant of a man so instead I just innocently sat down and began my scripted presentation. I had only spoken for a few minutes when Saul reclined back in his big leather chair, raised his hand and motioned me to stop.

"Son," he said. "Do you have any idea what it is you are trying to get me into?" He didn't wait for a reply but instead went right into telling me all the reasons why only a fool would invest in the Nevada Mining Industry. "It's worse than the strip" he said, referring to the gambling going on just up the street from his office.

I sat silently in my chair, having no ability to respond because, after all, I was young and just a go-fer. Saul continued on and on about the evils of the Gold mining industry. He told me it was full of crooks, false hopes, unrealistic dreams and dead ends. Having grown up in Nevada he had known many men who had lost their life's savings chasing the elusive yellow metal. He then went on to tell me some story about an ancient Asian king, the meaning of which still eludes me to this day, but the bottom line was--I should find a new line of work. Realizing I had no chance to create a lead here, I thanked him for his time and headed for the door.

"Wait a minute," Saul called out. "What is the minimum buy-in?"

"One Hundred Thousand," I replied.

"Count me in," He said.

Totally dumbfounded I asked why the sudden change of heart. He answered that he hadn't had any change of heart at all, but on the chance this deal hit the big time he didn't want to be the only one left out.

As I left his office that day, I thought and thought about the absurdity of the situation. "Why," I thought, "would someone with such a clear opinion as to the foolishness of this investment then turn around and put money into it?" It being money that he clearly expected to lose.

Upon returning to work I shared the experience with my boss. It was an experience that would be repeated many more times with businessmen, and women from many industries and professions. All seemed to have the same thing in common. Few believed they had much chance to make money in mining, yet all seemed willing to throw their own hard earned money into it.

I was particularly amazed at the medical profession. They seemed more willing than any to part with their money on the hopes of hitting the jackpot, though they openly admitted to knowing it was a long shot. I wondered how people of such a high level of education could make what seemed to be such foolish decisions.

These were the early years of forming my ideas about investing and investors, but I already was finding some great inconsistencies in the way people thought and acted.

My boss called it "gold fever." He said it made people do irrational things. He reminded me of the early gold rushes in this country and that very few people really made any money.

Most suffered great physical and emotional losses, yet for years the miners kept coming. The lure of fast riches drew them like a sickness into its grasp. They would leave good jobs and stable lives to come out west in search of their "pot of gold" even though they knew how great the odds were against them.

I didn't stay long with that company, but long enough to begin to form my ideas about investors and why they often made such foolish decisions. At the time I thought "gold fever" was purely related to mining, but have since learned it is an unbiased disease, willing to freely infect investors of all types.

Over the years I have watched so many investors make so many mistakes that I have taken to making note of the more common ones. What has amazed me most is that they usually know what they are doing is wrong. They can usually see the flaws in their thinking yet for whatever reasons choose to ignore it.

Ultimately I came to the conclusion that there are a series of myths upon which investors base their decisions. I use the word "myth" because the dictionary defines a myth as a "part truth that becomes and ideology." This is a key phrase. A "part truth" means there is some truth to it. It is much like the myths of ancient Greece which, though far-fetched in there descriptions of the workings of the gods, yet they are based on truths that were known at the time. Over the centuries the truths have been stretched and altered until they are hardly recognizable.

Thus a myth becomes a very dangerous thing. The part that is true makes the part that is not true more believable, and thus more dangerous. If I have a nice Chocolate milk shake with just a little bit of strychnine in it, it could be honestly said that most of the drink is good. But the part that is bad is deadly.

When we invest based on part truths, the part that is not true becomes the hidden poison that slowly kills off what good the rest may be doing. The good news about investing is that the myths may be discovered, and then removed. Of course the first step in discovering the myths is in understanding where most of them come from. The source may surprise you.

THE MYTHS
1 – Value

In December of 1999 I had been asked to participate in a panel of financial experts at a community event. It was two weeks before the dreaded turn of the century and our topic was "What is your biggest concern for Y2K?" Most will remember the panic that was overtaking the financial world at the time as we heard so many predictions about all the dire consequences that awaited us.

The event occurred in the setting of a luncheon, and so I found myself standing in a buffet line next to one of the regional managers of a top national brokerage firm. As we selected our food he began to talk to me about the markets, and to brag about how much money some of his clients were making in some stocks that were hot at the time. He named some top tech stocks of the day. Remember this was December of 1999. The dot.com bubble was full and at its peak.

I reminded him of some of the basics of financial planning that we both understood very well and asked if maybe he wasn't concerned that he was getting his clients into companies whose stocks were selling for far more than they may be worth. He just laughed and said "Oh Dan, if you are not in these stocks your clients are going to miss the boat. Old earnings formulas are no longer the issue because we are in a New Economy." I am sure many will remember that expression from those days. "The New Economy."

I replied to him that I wasn't sure his "boat" was one my clients would want to be on, and that as for the "New Economy," I was one who would always believe that a company's worth had to be reasonably related to its capacity to earn profits.

Though I had spent much of 1999 preaching against the "irrational exuberance" in the stock market, this comment hit me like a brick. I realized, perhaps for the first time, the source of many of the financial myths I had tried to warn my clients about. They were coming from the securities industry itself. Investment advisors, financial planners, analysts and supposed experts had lost sight of their own training and had gone on to believe in myths that they were then passing on to their unsuspecting clients.

I suspected his "boat" just may be the Titanic and I determined it was time to take my warnings to a higher level.

Shortly after this conversation, it was my turn to address the group. The other advisors had given their pre-approved speeches about Y2K and now the moderator asked me, "Mr. Wyson, what do you consider to be the greatest risk of Y2K?"

Since this event was being televised live I took the opportunity to look directly into the TV camera and said, "In my opinion, the greatest risk my friends, is not the computer issue. The greatest risk of Y2K is that your financial advisors have got you all buying stocks that are grossly overpriced. Our computer people will pull us through the turn of the century, but if you don't bring some common sense back to your investment decisions, then whether your computer works or not won't matter because you'll have no money left to track."

Feeling I had their attention I then went on to name a handful of examples. I am sure I hit on stocks that many in the audience were holding.

A stunned audience sat in silence as I returned to my seat. The event was recorded and rebroadcast so there was no question down the road what position I had taken. As to the timing I guess I got lucky, from a business point of view. But as to my message, it was absolutely true and the end result was inevitable. It was merely a matter of time.

The dot.com boom and bust of the late 90's was not the first time financial advisors have tried to convince us some new way of valuing investments has magically been invented, nor will it be the last. Like the gold rushers of the last century, people really want to believe money can be made faster and easier. In the end it always comes back to value. A company by definition is something that makes money. Either it must make money today, or have a reasonable likelihood of making money in the near future, but it must make money. Profits generate value and value drives stock prices over the long term. It is true that stocks go up and down in the short term with emotion, but it is my belief that in the long term, everything eventually returns to value.

The crash of 2000 would not be so bad if we had learned our lesson from all the billions of dollars lost. Unfortunately I do not think that is the case. Recently a stock came out on an IPO priced so high it scared many who still had 2000 fresh in their memories. Within the next couple of months that stock's price doubled in the market as analysts began to push the price targets higher and higher. Justifying his very high target one analyst responded that he knew it was very expensive, but compared to another company in the same industry that was also overpriced, it looked reasonable. In short he said that since other people were overpaying for some stocks, then buying this one was justified. Yep folks, lets just all hold hands and jump off the cliff together.

Myth: Earnings don't matter.

Truth: The ultimate goal of legitimate business is to make money – not just push its stock price up.

2 – It's Only Paper

I sat with a prospective client one day reviewing the holdings in her accounts as I routinely do. As I highlighted things of interest I came to one line with that familiar symbol – ENRN. When I went to line through it the lady protested almost as if she were protecting her own child.

"Don't do anything with my Enron!" She said with great emphasis.

I smiled and asked how much she had paid for her 400 shares. She was a little embarrassed to respond, "About $35,000."

On this particular day Enron was valued at eight cents per share, or roughly $32 for her entire position. She went on to tell me of all the sorrow that stock had given her and she was not quite willing to part with it yet. Then she said something I have heard a thousand times and expect to hear a thousand more. She told me that she understood from her prior advisor that you never really lose money until you sell. Until then, it is only a "paper loss."

Perhaps there is some level of truth to that statement if you are referring to tax issues, but otherwise this remains one of the top areas where investors like to fool themselves. This is also one of those myths that originates mostly from investment professionals themselves. Perhaps it is an attempt to buy time while the market recovers, rather than admit the obvious – that the client has lost money.

I am not one who believes you should look at your account values too often. Nor do I think it is wise to sell every position just because it is down. Going up and down is what stocks are prone to do. However, let's be honest with ourselves. If you bought a stock for $5 and now it is selling for $4, you lost $1.

It may very well be that you will get that dollar back. The stock may still be worth owning and maybe you even want to buy more of it. But it is still a fact that you lost $1. The question now is, what is the best way to move forward?

I turned to my prospect on the Enron stock and asked her a very pointed question. "If you had $32 today to invest would you buy Enron?"

"Of course not," she replied, "I am not stupid."

"Then why," I asked, "Do you keep holding it?"

I have never understood the concept analysts have of issuing a "hold" recommendation. In my mind if a stock is likely to go up I want to buy it. If it is not going anywhere, then I want to get rid of it. Where does "hold" come from? "Hold" I think must mean the analyst can't figure out what the stock is going to do so they basically issued a "no comment." Maybe we should change the rating then to "no comment."

As you look at your portfolio you have to ask yourself the question, "If I had this amount of money today would I buy these same positions?" If the answer is "no" then maybe you should consider making some changes. In effect, every day you "hold" a position, you are making a decision to buy it.

I do not encourage frequent trading in accounts. But I do encourage my clients to make sure they are not "holding" onto positions they are sorry they had only on the hope that they might go up. If you lost money, is it possible there is a better way to earn it back?

Money is paper. If you lose a $20 bill it is only a paper loss, but you will still be unhappy about it. If your account is down because of bad decisions, poor markets or just rotten luck, take a look at your positions and view them in the light of today's knowledge. Ask yourself these questions:

-Would I buy this today?
-Are the reasons I bought this stock still true?
-Is there a better investment available?

Don't hang on to losing positions as if they were your only child, just because you cannot emotionally bear to "take the loss." The loss is already there, in the past, so it is time to look to the future.

Myth: It's only a paper loss

Truth: If your account is worth less today than yesterday – it ***<u>is</u>*** *worth less today than yesterday.*

3 – Your Guess

Tom was in his mid 60's and as we reviewed his account it was clear he had fallen into many of the same traps as his fellow investors. During the boom years of the 90's he had made money like he could do no wrong. In fact almost everyone had. It is amazing how everyone is an expert when the market is going up every day.

The crash of 2000 hit and his account proceeded to lose over 60% of its value, effectively wiping out all those wonderful memories of his great prowess at picking stocks. He had come to my office, apparently humbled by the fall, in hopes of getting some advice on how to proceed. At least that is what he told me when he walked in.

As I reviewed his positions, and the process by which they came to be, he seemed to take a defensive stance on just about everything that came up. He was more interested in justifying his decisions than in trying to find a better solution for the future. The more he talked the more he convinced himself he had not made such poor decisions after all.

The discussion quickly reached a point where I no longer was doing any talking at all. I just sat back in my chair and listened, amazed at what I was hearing. The gentleman finally smiled and thanked me for my time and stood up to leave. As he walked out the door he turned to me and said, "Well, I think my guess is as good as anyone's."

I found myself analyzing that final comment for quite some time in light of the whole picture. First, the man had admittedly lost, through his own decisions, over 60% of his assets in a very short period of time. Secondly, he admitted by the comment itself that he really was only "guessing" and assumed everyone else was doing the same.

I recognize the wisdom of my clients who, after all, saved their money in the first place. However, I find it interesting that people who would never prescribe their own medical care, who would never perform their own dental surgery, or would never consider representing themselves in a court of law, still have no trouble making significant financial decisions for which they have had no training.

It is clear that in all the above professions, a certain level of uncertainty exists. To some degree, all professionals must exercise a certain level of "judgment" in their decisions, and they will not always be right. However, over time, a carefully thought out plan based on sound principals and a lifetime of experience dealing in similar matters, certainly makes the most sense.

Myth: My guess is as good as anyone's.

Truth: This is based on the assumption that your financial advisor is in fact, guessing. If that is truly the case then your proper course, rather than guess yourself, is to find an advisor who does not.

4 – Red Light Green Light

Kevin was so excited to call me and let me know about his latest "hot" idea for beating the market. He had been to a seminar which, from his description, seemed to sound more like an invitation to join multi-level marketing than a serious financial advice conference.

At this seminar Kevin learned about some great software. The promoters claimed to have the ability to predict the direction stocks were likely to move. Charting numerous factors and making complex calculations, this software would then make its picks and send them immediately to the subscribers of the service.

The picks would be displayed on the clients' computer screen in the form of green lights, meaning to buy, and red lights meaning to sell. Kevin was so excited because the system was so simple to operate. All he had to do was wait for the lights and then make his move. It sounded simple enough to me as well.

Kevin was so excited about his discovery. The software, which only cost a few thousand dollars, would quickly pay for itself based on the sponsor's estimates of 10-30% monthly returns. Of course there were many testimonials to "prove" results quoted were reasonable.

These seminars are not new, and dozens of versions of "red light, green light" software have been around since the advent of the PC. Prior to that the client would simply receive a phone call notifying them of the next hot move.

I asked Kevin to consider just a couple of basic realities before throwing his money into such a scheme. The first of which is the simple math involved. If an investment really can earn between 10 and 30% per month, it would not take long before even a modest investment would grow to billions of dollars. So now I ask this primary question: "If you had a computer program that could predict stocks and earn you billions of dollars in a very short period of time, why would you tell anyone else about it?"

John's reply should not have surprised me. He said the promoters made more money selling the software than using it. Hmm … I am sure that is a true statement, but for a different reason.

In all my years in financial services I must say I have had the opportunity to run into a few folks who developed systems for "beating the market" in a dramatic way. However, these same people are the last ones on earth to tell anyone what they are doing. Why in the world would they? Can you imagine the foolishness of a man at the horse track who has a hot inside tip on a horse, running around telling everyone else the good news? If he succeeded in getting hundreds of others to bet on the same horse, he would destroy the odds and cost himself any chance at a decent profit. If he really knew which horse was going to win, his most likely action would be to encourage others to bet on anything else.

Stock prices, and therefore stock profits, are based on a free market of supply and demand. When the green light hits and thousands of people on the "system" rush to buy a stock, there will likely be a temporary spike in the price. Like any "pyramid" plan, the first ones in will fare the best. However, since this spike is artificial and not based on real market changes, it more often than not will fall faster than it rose.

Consider for a moment who really could benefit from a "green light-red light" system? If you guessed the person who knows what light is going to come out 5 minutes before it does, you will begin to understand where the real profits are in these systems.

A good financial advisor does not profess to have some secret system for obtaining unreasonable returns. She is someone who seeks to obtain reasonable returns for you within your appropriate level of risk.

There is a difference between serious experts who write books on how to invest intelligently, and less-than-credible operators who, in most cases, are trying to sell you a "quick wealth" system that never worked for them in the first place.

The mindset of these people is very simple. Develop a system and if it works they will make a fortune – if it doesn't work they can sell it to someone else.

Myth: People who have figured out how to beat the market are happy to sell their secrets to me.

Truth: When someone finds a buried treasure the last thing they want to do is tell the world where it is.

5 – A Taxing Issue

It has been said the greatest expense anyone has in their lifetime is taxes. It might be a mistake to invest solely to avoid or reduce taxes, but certainly taxes need to be seriously considered in every investment decision.

Consider the case of Louise. In her early 80's she was interested in finding a comfortable second home closer to her children. The area was reasonably priced and she found a small but adequate condo for about $120,000. The next morning Louise called her broker of 10 years and asked if he would draw the money off a very large annuity she owned to pay for the condo. The broker immediately placed the order and the check was sent out.

Louise paid cash for her condo and enjoyed it immensely for the next 8 months until her CPA called with a disturbing tax question.

You see the $120,000 Louise had pulled from the annuity represented almost all gains. Since the IRS views annuities as LIFO, last in first out, the money to come out first are the fully taxable earnings. This move had added almost $120,000 to Louise's taxable income for the prior year. The CPA wanted to know how she intended on paying the taxes, calculated at nearly $60,000.

The sad part of this story is that Louise had more tax efficient options for generating the money she needed. One might ask who was in the wrong here. Was it her advisor? Clearly he should have had the wisdom to properly advise her to consider the tax consequences of her decision to sell the annuity. In the strictest sense however, he had taken her order and placed it as requested. He was following his client's instructions.

Maybe Louise was at fault for not asking more questions. Could she be expected to know the tax consequences of her decisions or does she have the right to assume her advisor should say something if he had a problem with it?

In any case, on the day Louise's situation was brought to me for advice, the damage had been done and could not be taken back. That is often the case when dealing with tax issues.

Similar dramatic consequences happen when people miss their IRA required minimum distribution.

While speaking with a client about a recommendation, I brought up the tax issue and he immediately cut me off and said, "Dan, taxes are secondary – I never base my investment decisions on them." I reminded him that we live in a society where total taxes often exceed 50% and to not consider them anytime you move money around can lead to disaster.

Myth: Taxes are a secondary decision.

Truth Taxes may be secondary to sound investing, but no decisions should ever be made without considering them. Taxes in investing are like mosquitoes on a humid summer day. The less attention you give to them, the more blood they will take.

6 – Losing Interest

You commonly hear the phrase, "You don't have to be a rocket scientist to know that." I have a friend who just happens to be that rocket scientist most people don't need to be. Therefore it seems appropriate that he is also one of the few people I have met in my career who already was well aware of myth number six.

While visiting him one day and walking around his nice ranch type property where he lives, he commented about the improvements he was making to the kitchen area. Things were moving along well enough but not as quickly as he would have liked. When I asked the cause of the delay he mentioned he did not want to go into debt for it, as his home was paid for, so they were building on a "pay-as-you-go" method. This intrigued me since I was fully supportive of his plan, but such an attitude was so rare in our buy-first, pay-later culture.

"Don't you want to have a big mortgage like everyone else so you can get the tax deduction?" I asked. His reply was what I have told people for years. "You know Dan, it is cheaper to pay 35% in taxes than 100% in interest."

He went on to explain that if he paid $10,000 in home mortgage interest, he could deduct it from his gross income and save about $3,500 in taxes based on his tax bracket. He then turned the question back on me and asked, "Doesn't it make sense to just pay the $3,500 to the IRS rather than the $10,000 to the mortgage company?"

It was such simple math yet it always amazes me how many people never think about it. I know of some CPA's who actually encourage people to incur debt to reduce their taxes. When I have asked about this policy, the question has usually created some discomfort in the tax professional and eventually a hesitant admission that living debt-free probably is the best financial position to take. Of course we must remember we go to a tax professional to get ideas on how to save on taxes. Sometimes they give us just what we ask for, but if saving on taxes costs us more in the end, maybe we should reconsider our priorities.

I have had a handful of clients in my life who despise the IRS so much they have told me they would rather burn $1000 than give ten bucks to the government. If this is the case, I guess an expensive mortgage works as well as anything.

Myth: Interest is cheaper than taxes

Truth: Don't get so caught up in avoiding taxes (see myth #5) that you lose sight of what is best for you financially.

7 – Risk Free

An ad in a local paper blared out the following claim: "CD's – the Risk Free way to invest."

Certainly when you work mainly with people in retirement you are bound to come across a lot of government insured products; Cd's, Treasury Bills and Bonds, savings accounts and the like. In fact you would be disappointed if you didn't since people who have left the work force should naturally seek a lower level of risk in their investments.

A proper definition of risk would be appropriate at this time as it relates to money. Risk, represents the likelihood of loss. If someone has no chance at all of loss then they are said to have no risk.

CD's sold by banks which carry FDIC insurance are often considered to be without risk to principal. This is due to the fact that the FDIC is backed by the U.S. Government with its almost unlimited taxing ability. Obviously no government can claim that it will last forever, but for the sake of modern investing, U.S. backed instruments are said to be without risk to loss of principal. But are they really?

There are many different types of risk in investing. Some of the more common are:

<u>Market risk</u> – the risk that the market will move against you.

<u>Credit risk</u> – the risk that the entity you have invested in will have financial troubles.

<u>Policy risk</u> - the risk that a government will enact new laws that will work against your investment.

None of these seem to affect the government insured products, but what about inflation risk? The risk that inflation will erode your principal? Simply put, if you earn 3% per year and inflation moves to 6% per year, then even though your principal is guaranteed in theory, in reality your principle will lose 3% of its value every year.

Inflation has been kept under reasonable control in recent years, but citizens of many other countries can tell you that inflation is often the greatest financial risk they have to deal with. Money locked up in a "guaranteed" account for several years during a time of high inflation, can be riskier in many cases than an alternative "non-government insured" product.

This is not to say you should not use CD's which have FDIC insurance, or Treasury Bonds and Bills. They have a good place in your portfolio. But don't fall prey to the myth that "Government insured products have no risk."

I have a friend who keeps his entire estate, several million dollars, in "government insured" products. He does so because he does not want "any risk" to his principle. The reality is that he is at risk to inflation eroding his assets. Sometimes it helps to remind ourselves that there really is nothing in life that is totally "risk-free" and financial planning becomes a process as much focused on managing risk as on managing money.

Myth-Government insured products are risk-free.

Truth-You can never totally eliminate risk from anything in life, but you can manage it.

8 – Not Afraid to Lose

The first thing I do when I new person walks into my office is try and get a feel about their attitudes towards life, their goals, and their money. There is no "perfect" way to invest just like there is no perfect entrée in any restaurant. For every person who just loves the Rigatoni, there will be someone else who for whatever reason would prefer a juicy steak, or garden salad.

We are all different. We have different dreams. We have different fears. My job is to find a person's values and try to help them build an investment plan around them.

As I conduct my initial interview one question I commonly ask, and the one which elicits the strangest looks, is "how much money are you willing to lose this year?" Clients are so accustomed to having advisors talk about how much money they are going to make, it startles them to be asked about losing.

The answer inevitably comes back, "None. I am not willing to lose any money this year."

One lady I met with recently, I will call her Joanne, went so far as to say she fretted and lost sleep over even a $5 dip in her account. By the way, she had a very large account.

When I then turn to look at the investments in the account, I often feel like I am in a fast food restaurant visiting with someone across the table who is gorging themselves on their "supersized" meal, while explaining to me how important a healthy lifestyle is.

As I said, it is not my job to find the perfect investment, or to tell someone what to do with his or her money. It is my job to discover what people want, and in many cases guide them along as they discover for themselves what they want, and then help them to obtain it in an intelligent manner. It could be said it is my job to create consistency between what people want from their money, and what they are actually doing with it.

As I reviewed Joanne's account I found she had about half her money invested where the volatility was actually very high. I estimated that she could lose about 30% of her portfolio in any one year. She then laughed as she told me that was almost exactly what she had lost in the past market downturn. Her presence in my office was evidence of her displeasure with her current situation.

I explained to Joanne that I have found most people, in investing, err on the side of danger. The amount their account is set up to potentially lose, is usually far greater than the amount they tell me they are "willing" to lose. It is this common inconsistency in accounts that results in so much lost sleep and stressful "down" days in the market.

No one can predict the direction of the markets since there are so many variables. It is possible though, using historic measures, to design an account that is likely to stay within certain parameters. That is to say, we don't know when it is going to rain, or how much, but we can get an idea of how much rain has historically fallen, and build a home that can handle it. We can also have a backup plan in case a rainstorm goes beyond what is normal, while still putting in enough windows to benefit from the sunlight we know will eventually return.

As was the case with Joanne, it is usually the case that most people build a financial home with inadequate planning for the storms. They know they don't want too much risk, and they know how badly they feel when they lose money, but still they invest as if they expect storm clouds to never gather.

Myth:" I don't mind taking a little risk".

Truth: No one really wants to lose money, yet many invest with far more risk than they are aware of.

9 – Great Returns

What most people want is not obtainable. They want a high rate of return with no risk. It is sometimes a difficult process emotionally when I show the "Real" risk in an account that an individual is taking in their attempts to get that high rate of return.

Money is a commodity, like sugar or corn or pork bellies. (I had to sneak pork bellies in here somewhere because the whole expression always elicits such an interesting image) Like all commodities its price is based on supply and demand. The more someone needs your money, and the fewer people there are that are willing to give it, the more that person is willing to pay you to get it.

For example, if I am a major world wide corporation with a fantastic credit rating and lots of assets to back me up, I will find an unlimited number of entities interested in loaning me money. Therefore, I can put it out to the lowest bidder and obtain that investment money at a very low rate.

If I am trying to start a brand new high tech business with no history and just a desk full of dreams, inevitably I will need to offer a much greater return to attract investment money away from a more established company.

In all this it pays to remember basic human nature. Everyone wants a bargain and no one is going to pay more for your money than they have to.

I often get clients in my office asking about the Trust Deeds they see advertised on highway billboards that pay high rates of return and offer full protection of principal. I ask them to consider two simple questions.

#1 – Would any developer pay 12% to borrow money from you if they could borrow it elsewhere for 11%?

#2 – Why are they not able to borrow at 11%?

They always think for a moment and then the smile comes to their face. “Oh, I get it,” they say. How funny is it that the same investors who would drive across town to save twelve cents on a gallon of milk, somehow think investment firms with great credit and strong backing are somehow willing to pay twice for money what it is worth? The reality is, they are not. They pay more because they have to.

When a company offers an above market return, try to discover why they have to pay so much, and then determine if the investment fits within your personal goals. Trust Deeds and the like may well be a great investment, but do your due diligence first so you will know what you are buying.

Myth: I can get lucky and find a high return with no risk.

Truth: If you see a "fire sale" on money, stop and ask yourself why no one else wants to buy it.

10 – Low Cost Retirement

This myth does not apply so much to investing as it does to the ultimate goal of why we do it.

I have had the privilege over the years of working with many fine individuals. We have come to call them the "greatest generation" because they struggled through difficult times of our nation's history and came out on top. They know much of sorrow, sacrifice and patience. They have learned the good things in life require planning and discipline to obtain.

Now free from their prior obligations to "earn" a living, these people spend their time in what we call "retirement." That is a word that has changed very much in the past few decades.

Retirement does not just mean not having to work anymore. It also means pursuing lifelong dreams of travel, hobbies, talents and socializing in all their various forms. It means visiting children and the always-loveable grandchildren. These kids no longer live down the block but with our new world are often found spread all over the country.

Retirement also means an aging body with new aches, new diseases and daily needs. It means higher taxes in many cases. Yes, you read that correctly. When the government "sold" the IRA program, one of its pillars was the accepted truth that taxes would be lower in old age. Well, with no mortgage, no children, and often-high investment income from a lifetime of saving, it is surprising how many retired people are in the highest tax bracket of their lives.

All of this new definition of retirement boils down to one great need – money. Too many people create their savings plan based on the false assumption that financial needs will be lower in retirement. The reality is that spending is often much higher.

There are many retirement calculators that assume you will need only 60-70% of your pre-retirement income to maintain your level of living. I advise my clients to do the math, be realistic about how they expect to live, and plan accordingly. The school lunches you no longer need to buy can be quickly replaced by skyrocketing medical needs as your body begins to wear down. In planning for retirement it is wise to assume your current standard of living will require as much cash flow then as it does now – adjusted for inflation of course. If it turns out you are able to live comfortably on less, then all the better. At least you will have a safety net.

Myth: I will need less money in retirement.

Truth: Maybe. Maybe not.

11 – Plaid Suits

In my office I have a cartoon of a man stranded on a deserted island, emaciated and almost dead from hunger and thirst. Along comes a luxury yacht with a man on the bow wearing a plaid suit and holding a briefcase. The caption points out that the man is not coming to save the castaway, but merely to sell him some needed typhoon insurance.

This cartoon typifies the way we have come to see insurance salesmen. On our list of people we don't trust, the insurance sales person typically falls some distance below used car salesmen. Their reputation is not entirely undeserved, as many have made their livelihood with one hand shaking ours while the other was picking our pockets. At the same time the entertainment industry has done much to perpetuate this image.

The insurance industry clearly has an image problem and has made a constant effort to teach its agents to sell insurance without looking like insurance salesmen. They call themselves by many names, one of the most common being "financial planner." Few professional titles are more abused than that of Financial Planner. Only a small percentage of Advisors carry the designation of CERTIFIED FINANCIAL PLANNER®, but that doesn't stop the rest from claiming the title.

My main concern with the whole insurance image is the damage done to the consumer by this perception. Some people have developed such a negative connotation of "insurance salesmen" that they have attached that same feeling to the products they carry.

Insurance is one of those challenging products that you hate to pay for, but you can't afford to not have. So often I will hear people say something like this. "I put money into that life policy for years and never got a dime back." My natural response is, "Would you be happier if you could have made a claim?"

A wise approach to take towards insurance is to separate the salesperson from the product. Don't deny yourself needed coverage, or some of the wonderful benefits available through insurance products, just because you have come to distrust the people who sell them.

Some common missed opportunities are:

Life Insurance as an estate-planning tool.

A commonly overlooked estate planning tool is "second to die" life insurance. A policy of this type is designed to cover two lives, and pays only when the second of the two dies. If positioned properly in a life insurance trust, commonly called an ILIT, the policy can leverage a small amount of dollars into a fairly large payout at death. This payout is often federal, state and estate tax-free. This allows you to pass, outside of your estate, a large amount of money to your heirs. This money passes immediately upon death and in addition to avoiding taxes, is usually not subject to probate. When someone dies, often the first money their heirs see is the life insurance proceeds.

Long Term Care.

There is a potential here to make many mistakes so please consult a trusted advisor. The main complaint with LTC is that it is so expensive. When you consider that the likelihood of filing a claim is almost 50%, you begin to understand why the insurance company *must* charge so much for the coverage.

Long term care insurance is not for everyone. If you have substantial assets you may just want to self-insure. If you have minimal assets you have to decide if you can really afford the premiums. There is a window of assets and if you fall within this window you become a good candidate for this type of coverage. Remember that in a marriage situation the greatest risk is for the first person to need the care, since it will require you to maintain two separate households. If you live alone and own your own home, you have the option of selling your home to pay for the coverage.

Annuities.

This is far too large a topic for the purposes of this book. Annuities, like most insurance products have a correct and an incorrect application. Used correctly they can provide guarantees and tax advantages. Used incorrectly they can become an expensive and restrictive product. Make sure you understand the fine print before you buy.

One of the biggest problems I find with annuities is the agents selling them often do not understand the intricacies of the products, so they cannot explain them to you. This is understandable since some are very complicated. Yet used correctly, there can be many good benefits in using annuities for a portion of your retirement planning.

Because the commissions on some annuities can be high, I recommend getting a second opinion from an advisor other than the one who stands to benefit from selling you the annuity.

Myth: Insurance salesmen all wear plaid suits.

Truth: Insurance products, if used correctly, can offer benefits to your retirement plan that you cannot find anywhere else.

12 – Stirring the Pot

When I was young I loved to cook. My mom would often give me little pointers along the way. Some made a lot of sense to me and others were not so clear. One thing that always seemed a mystery was why I could not stir the pancake batter until it was nice and smooth. "Don't stir it up too much," she would remind me, "just enough to blend the ingredients and not one bit more."

Being a young child with lots of curiosity I decided one day, when my mom was out of the kitchen, to stir the batter my way. When I was finished it was the finest looking, smoothest pancake batter our home had ever seen. I was so proud. Surely this would make pancakes as beautiful as the batter.

As you may have guessed, my beautiful batter spread out all over the pan, resulting in a very thin, very flat, and very unappetizing breakfast. As soon as my mom saw it she said, "Danny, you stirred it up too much."

Investors find themselves in my similar situation on a regular basis. They search until they find the perfect financial recipe. Then they carefully measure out all the ingredients; a little of this and a little of that, topped off with a dash of the other. Then they begin to stir it all together, and they stir and they stir and they stir. They walk away for a moment and then, unable to control the need to be in control, they stir it up again.

As with my pancakes, the result is often flat and unappetizing. Evidence of this phenomenon is a study conducted some years ago in which it was discovered that the average investor only earned a fraction of the market average. What was the explanation for these results? It was the inability of investors to avoid "stirring things up" too much. The recipe was a good one, but people just couldn't resist the temptation to stick their fingers back in it.

There is a time to make changes in your portfolio, but more often than not the temptation is to change things too often. Markets follow cycles and any good investment plan takes cycles into consideration. If you have 4 investments and three are up while one is down, do not automatically assume the down one is bad and needs to be sold. You must consider the long term design of your portfolio and see if it is still consistent with your goals.

I like to ask my clients how often they check the values in their portfolios. When they tell me more than once a week I get concerned. When they tell me everyday, I get very concerned. I want to make sure I am not dealing with someone who, at the first sign of trouble in the markets, is going to run in with the spoon and want to stir the batter. It's always frustrating when you take the time to formulate a long term plan for someone, and then two months later they call to tell you that you should sell the one position in four that happens to be down. They fail to understand that every ingredient is important, and plays a part in the overall plan.

Numerous studies have shown that there is an inverse relationship between the amount of trades in an account, and the growth rate. That is to say, as a general but not specific rule, the more someone trades the less money they make.

Of course your advisor should follow your investments on a continual basis to assure they still meet the goals of the original plan. But investors would do well to spend more time golfing and shopping and less time trying to implement myth number 12.

Myth: When things aren't going just right I should fix it.

Truth: Don't try to manage a 10-year financial plan with 1-month decisions.

13 – Fee or Free

As the world of financial advice matures, the choices of advisors continues to widen, as does the advice on how to choose one. Currently, there is a popular mantra out there that teaches it is better to hire a "fee-based" advisor rather than use a commission based one because you will get more objective advice.

Before I offer my opinion on this current topic let me state that I am licensed for "fee-based" planning in the states in which I do business. Therefore when a client enters my office I can offer either a fee, or a commission based service. It really doesn't matter to me so long as I can be fairly compensated for my efforts. I am sure none of my clients are foolish enough to believe I work for free, and in reality many express concern that I be paid enough for the planning I do for them. They recognize the value of the services of a financial advisor.

So the question becomes, "Will I get better advice from a fee-based or commission based advisor?" Generally the feeling is that a fee-based advisor will give you more unbiased advice. I believe that assumption is based on a faulty premise. It assumes, at the outset, that your commission based advisor lacks integrity and is willing to put you in a product that is more in his best interest than in yours. If you really believed your advisor had integrity, you wouldn't worry about how he got paid, because you would know he was doing first and foremost what is best for you.

So let's assume that premise is correct. Ie. Financial advisors lack integrity so we need to use fee-based planning to keep them in line. Well, what are we saying? We are saying that we cannot trust the people who are advising us in our major financial decisions. If that is true, then why use them at all? I don't know about you but if my commission based advisor cannot be trusted to give me the best advice, then why would I feel better paying him by the hour?

On the other hand, if my fee-based advisor is a person of great integrity who is interested in helping me make the most of my financial positions, then why do I care whether that advisor is paid by the hour or through commissions? In either case the money comes out of my pocket and in both cases I am confident I will be treated fairly.

One day while discussing business matters with my Dad, I commented that if he paid his employees more they would probably work harder. He replied that nothing was further from the truth. "People," he said, "have integrity or they do not. You cannot pay them to acquire it." He went on to explain that paying more money might bring in a higher level of employee, but on any individual level he had learned in his businesses that people work hard because they are hard workers. And people goof off, because they are goof-offs, and wages do not affect that.

Financial planners are people too. Some are honest and some are not. Fortunately I have found in many years of business that most financial advisors really do act in the best interest of their clients. They really do try to do the best thing for them. The main difference between advisors lies more in skills and qualifications than anything else. When I have seen a problem with commission based advisors it has often been with ones who only had one product to sell.

When I come across a poor plan, it is less due to lack of integrity and more to lack of understanding than anything else. The financial world is a complicated one, and to stay on top of it requires daily, (I did say daily) study and effort. Advisors, who do not constantly keep on top of the game, find themselves giving their clients poor, or outdated advice.

Now back to the issue at hand. If the main difference in advisors is related to their financial education and skills – then a poorly trained advisor is not going to give you any better advice on a fee-basis than a commission basis. It won't matter how you pay him. The advice will be the same.

This is not to say fee-based planning does not make sense in many situations. I merely wanted to point out another myth – which as you remember is defined as a "part truth" – upon which people improperly make their decisions.

Myth: A fee-based planner will do a better job for me. Myth part 2-Some advisors work for free.

Truth: All advisors get paid. The most important factor is to find one who is honest, and well qualified to handle your particular situation.

Addendum:

Many advisors who focus on insurance products like to say that their services are "free to the client" because the insurance company pays their wages. That makes about as much sense as a car salesman pretending the size of his commission has no impact on the price of the car.

All employees of all companies have their wages ultimately paid for by the customers of that company. A fee-based platform can be good because the client will know exactly what they are paying for the service they receive, but in the end, what really matters is the quality of the advisor. There are great advisors on both sides of this issue.

14 – Trusts are for the Rich

It is pretty common for people to ask me about trusts and estates and such. Often the entire decision as to whether to have the trust or not is based on whether our estate is large enough to fall under the current estate tax limits. The trouble is that congress keeps messing with the numbers. Planning your death around the current estate tax laws is a risky game you are bound to lose.

My advice here is simple. In my business I lose all my clients to death—yep—they all die on me. A properly written trust and well-planned estate makes that event so much easier on your heirs. There is no need for some judge to decide how to divide your property because the trust already owns it, and your successor trustee just takes over.

I wonder sometimes when people complain to me about how much it costs to setup an estate through an attorney. Let me just say it is substantially cheaper than it will cost if you don't do it. I advise people to see a trust attorney because it is in their best interests. The fee you pay today, though it may seem excessive, years from now will be miniscule compared to the grief it avoids for your heirs.

Trusts are not about saving taxes. Trusts are about providing a way for assets to pass from one generation to the next without hassles and with minimal expense. The trust kicks in at a time in life when your heirs are grieving and usually not in a position to make difficult financial decisions. Do your kids a favor and make these decisions for them in advance, during a time of clear thought and calm emotions.

I am not an attorney so I do not give legal advice, but I always recommend people see a good trust attorney and obtain some qualified guidance.

Myth: Trusts are for the rich

Truth: Trusts are for anyone who wants to make their passing easier and less expensive to their children.

15 – Buy Low

A good friend and I recently had a wonderful visit. He is in his late 70's and has pretty much done it all when it comes to investing. He was a risk taker who loved to chase after the next big score. His "everything on red" attitude had cost him millions in lost earnings over the course of his life.

In the humility and honesty of old age, he looked back and realized how much better off he would be had he just followed a simple and well thought out plan. He was impatient, and impatience led him to try to make too much, too fast.

"I thought it would be easy" he said. "All I had to do to get rich in the market was to buy low and sell high. Unfortunately," he said, "I never seemed to be able to figure out where the "high" and the "low" were."

The "buy-low-sell-high" mentality has ruined many a fortune. In concept it sure makes a lot of sense but like most myths, it just doesn't work that way. At least it doesn't work that way in real life. We can always look back on any investment and find the "buy" and "sell" points where a substantial amount of gain could have been made. But as we look forward it is very difficult to find these same points. The trouble with this mentality is it creates investors who are forever trying to time just where the "low" point is, then when they have profits they are afraid to sell for fear they might miss the best "high."

In many ways financial planning resembles the practice of medicine. We take your temperature, look into your eyes, ears and mouth, tap on your knees a few times and ask you how you feel. Then, based on past experience with similar patients we attempt to provide a proper diagnosis and treatment.

As is the case with medicine, there is often a need to alter the prescription as we go forward. There is sometimes a call for further examination of the situation.

You cannot predict with certainty where markets will go or what world conditions will be from day to day. That is why the financial doctor gets up every morning and reviews the charts. If he sees something new, he gives you a call. If not, then at least he has you come in annually for a check-up.

Over the course of many years the end result should be an investment account that grows to keep up with your needs and goals. It does so because your doctor knows that even though he will be wrong some of the time, he will also be correct enough of the time that things will work out just fine.

Buying low and selling high is a dream that needs to be replaced with a well thought out plan to buy at a reasonable price and sell at a reasonable gain somewhere down the road.

Myth: Buy low and sell high to make money.

Truth: Buy smart and avoid greed. Sell when you can take the fair profits you need to reach your goals.

16 – Financial Experts

The media is full of experts anxious to share their financial wisdom with all who will listen. I get the opportunity on a regular basis to be "instructed" by my clients on some new thing they learned on the prior nights' financial show, or in some periodical.

I have no problem at all with this instruction, as I believe we should spend a fair amount of our time learning good things that benefit our lives. Personally I try to spend at least 20% of my business time in education.

Understanding complicated investment options presents some unique challenges. I am fairly certain that for any financial point of view, you can find someone equally intelligent with the complete opposite position.

You may note that the longest running financial programs feature two-sides and a moderator. One person may believe we are headed for higher inflation and they make a strong case for their position. Then someone with equal credentials begins to explain why deflation is eminent. As an audience we wonder who to believe, and which course to follow. Of course if we have a good advisor she can show us how to position our account for either possibility.

A client came in my office holding an article which discussed in detail all the reasons why retired folk should not invest in the stock market. I smiled and pulled out an article from a leading financial magazine which said it was time for America's seniors to get back in the market. Both articles were intelligent and well thought out. But how do you know which to believe?

As is often the case in life, the truth lies somewhere in the middle. It is not that all these experts don't know what they are talking about, because they certainly have done their homework. It is more a matter of them not knowing "whom" they are talking to.

Imagine listening to a doctor on the radio discuss some strange disease. Finding you have some of the symptoms you immediately run out to the pharmacy and buy the necessary prescription. Of course you couldn't do this because the medical profession recognizes the need for an individual evaluation.

The same is true in the practice of financial medicine. General concepts can be discussed and possible solutions reviewed, but each person needs to seek out individual answers to questions that are as personal as your physical health.

It is common for me to hear the phrase, "I listen to so-and-so on the radio and do what he tells me." So-and-so may be a very intelligent advisor but without knowing your individual situation, the best he can do is give very generalized advice. One of the most important rules of financial planning is to "know your client."

Myth: If an advisor has a national TV or Radio show he obviously is better than the financial guy down the street.

Truth: The best advisor in the world cannot give you any real solutions unless they know your unique situation.

17 – Charity or Not

A cute couple stopped by my office and asked about various opportunities for charitable giving. They had heard about CRT's, CRUT's,, CLT's and PCT's and wanted to know the difference between them all.

As the discussion progressed I quickly came to understand this couple was not so much interested in the charity concept as the desire to find a way to avoid taxes.

You often hear about the super wealthy who start family foundations so they can keep all their assets out of the hands of the tax collector. Charitable opportunities are often sought out as a way to take part in some benefit assumed to be left only to the super rich. Somehow we have in our mind that these elite individuals can just put money into a trust, and then pay no more taxes on it. It is really much more complicated than that.

Dozens of books could be written on this topic so let me just say one or two things about it. There is a point of wealth, past which, you have more money than you and all your heirs could ever spend. It is really true that you can only spend so much money in your lifetime. Beyond that amount, the acquisition of wealth is more about "controlling" money than about spending it. When the super wealthy start family foundations, they may technically be setting it aside for tax purposes, but it doesn't matter to them because they, and their heirs, still continue to control it.

For the average person seeking charitable opportunities I always point out first that "charity" is *charity*. First and foremost it means giving up something so that another may benefit by it. Now in the process there will likely be some tax benefits, but the net result is still a financial loss to the donor. If you give away $1 to save 50 cents in taxes, you are still out net 50 cents. The belief that you can give $1 to charity and receive $2 in tax benefits, is not only fallacious, but it is legally dangerous.

Charitable giving is an American tradition and a worthy venture. When doing so, focus on the benefit to others and let any tax benefit to yourself be a pleasant by-product. If your goal is to get a bigger tax advantage than the gift you are giving, then consider your motivations and whether or not you want to spend your nights worrying about the tax auditor knocking on your door.

Myth: You can enrich yourself financially with the tax benefits of charitable giving.

Truth: You will enrich yourself in non-financial ways when you freely share what you have with others less fortunate.

18 – Stocks Are Too Risky for Retirees

There is a natural tendency for humans to go to extremes. Nowhere is this more obvious than in dietary fads. Years ago it became quite popular to be critical of dairy products. Because of certain risks of eating dairy, many eliminated it completely from their diets. For a while those caught up in the fad felt pretty good about themselves, until they started developing other health issues resulting from the lack of the good vitamins and minerals that dairy had to offer. And so the fad blew over and people went back to milk, cheese and eggs, in moderation.

Then came the anti-salt movement. Once again people went to great lengths to eliminate all salt from their diet. In time, like the anti-dairy fad, we quickly learned that salt is a valuable part of our diet, in moderation. Carbs, fats, sugars and dozens more have all taken their turn on the anti-wagon, each with the same general result. Eventually we learn that by totally eliminating all risks associated with a certain food, we also deprive ourselves of the benefits those same foods hold for us. And so the phrase prevails; all things in moderation.

It should come as no surprise that fad chasing infects investors as well. Throughout economic cycles people have moved from one investment fad to another, in many cases with the same results as their changing diets. They avoid products known to carry certain risks, and in the process deprive themselves of the benefits those same products have to offer.

Since the stock market crash of 2008 it has become popular for some financial advisors to proclaim that no senior citizen should have any money in the stock market. I suppose since the crash involved real estate as well, these same advisors might want to recommend all seniors get rid of their homes. The anti-market fad has led many to tie their money up in long term products promoted as being safe from all market risk. What the fad fails to recognize is that while it might successfully avoid one risk, it exposes its followers to new ones.

There is no doubt that the stock market carries investment risk. There is also no doubt that many Americans suffered real estate losses as a result of the crash. But as I look over the financial condition of hundreds of my clients, I see a recurring theme. That is that over the many decades of their lives, and through multiple investment cycles, in the end the bulk of their current wealth resulted from the stock and bond markets and their real estate holdings.

I love milk, cheese, eggs and even salt. I recognize there are risks associated with eating any of them. I also realize there are benefits to be obtained from all of them. Investing is no different. Those who chase fads will face new risks. Those who recognize the benefit of using many different tools in moderation, in my personal experience, stand the best chance of a healthy financial life.

Myth: Stocks are too risky for senior investors

Truth: Individual investors should assess their individual needs and invest accordingly.

19 – Why Look to the Past?

There is an interesting contradiction in the marketing of most investment products. Almost all carry a disclaimer that states something like this: "Past returns are no guarantee of future performance."

They then go on to tell you what the past returns have been in a manner clearly designed to imply that they really do indicate what the future performance will be.

So if the past really is not indicative of the future, then why bring it up? If it does show what you can expect down the road, then why the disclaimer?

I am reminded of a meeting I had with a senior manager one day while working for a national brokerage firm. I was seeking permission to speak to a group of teachers at a convention and planned on talking about financial matters. Since ours is an industry of laws, regulations and most importantly, litigation, any information presented to the public must be pre-approved prior to use. My manager was quizzing me about what I planned on saying and whether there would be any handouts. The more he quizzed, the more frustrated I became.

Frustration with this part of the industry is common for most advisors. Finally I stood up and said in a less than controlled voice, "O.K. Let me get this straight. I can say whatever I want so long as I don't write it down, don't hand anything out, don't let anyone record it, don't make any promises and don't discuss any topic that involves money in any form." The manager sat quietly for a moment and then he blurted out, "Exactly." We both then laughed.

Of course we were being sarcastic but the exchange was an example of the challenges of working in an industry where regulations require so much scrutiny of any information that is given to the public. We want the public to be properly informed, but often restrictions can result in less information being shared, rather than more, as advisors are sometimes unwilling to go through all the hoops necessary to get information approved. Where this challenge becomes most concerning is that many of the rules regarding communication with the public only apply to those who are licensed to sell securities. This opens the door for unlicensed individuals to offer unregistered products with little or no scrutiny.

And so we work in an industry where there are so many disclaimers on everything it is amazing the clients are ever able to make a decision. As for past performance, it is certainly true that past performance can be no guarantee of future results. However, it is equally true that an educated investor should consider past performance as one of the many pieces of information that can help to formulate an informed decision.

Myth: Past performance is no guarantee of future results.

Truth: Though the myth is true, past performance is still an important tool in evaluating an investment.

20 – Fuzzy Math

With my computer it is possible to run what are known as "hypotheticals." This is a chart that shows how an investment would have performed over a past number of years.

For example, if you owned four different mutual funds, the hypothetical would show you in real dollars how that portfolio would have actually performed over a certain period of time. This is useful because it will not only show the average rate of return, but it will more importantly show you how it would have done during the bad times.

It is easy and fun to make money when markets are hot, but often a more important consideration is to know what your investments would do if the markets turn cold. For example, how would the funds you are buying today have performed during the market crash of 2000 or 2007? Or the prior two recessions?

The hypothetical will give you a feel for the potential downside of your investments if a similar situation arises in the future.

While doing a hypo with a client, he asked if I would replace one of the mutual funds I had selected with one of his choice that had a historical return of about 4% higher than the one I had chosen. It is common for investors to judge funds by their historical rates of return, thinking that the best returns are the most desirable. This seems to make sense.

I told him, based on my knowledge of his fund, that it would hurt the portfolio. Of course he did not believe me so I plugged it in and ran the program.

Sure enough, the total return of the entire portfolio over the past 20 years came in almost two percent lower. My client was confused and struggled to understand how this could be so. Upon reviewing the hypo year by year, we discovered that in 3 bad market periods, his fund fell dramatically and pulled the entire portfolio down with it. In these poor years the portfolio lost much more money than in the hypo I had run for him.

What was the result? It has been wisely said that the most important rule in investing is to first lose no money. This is because it is so difficult to recover from losses based on the math of investing. Let me give you a simple example.

If I have $100,000 and gain 20 %, I would then have $120,000. If I then lost 10% I would have $108,000. As follows:

$100,000 X 1.20 = $120,000
$120,000 X .9 = $108,000

One might ask what is the average rate of return in this example. To calculate that you add up the two rates of return and divide by the number of years.

$$\begin{array}{l} +20\% \\ \underline{+(-10\%)} \\ = 10\% \div 2 = 5\% \end{array}$$

So we have a 5% average rate of return. But is it really? Let's take the same $100,000 and grow it at 5% annually for two years.

$100,000 X 1.05 = $105,000
$105,000 X 1.05 = $110,250

How is it possible that in the first example you have $108,000 after two years while in the second example you have $110,250 yet the mathematical rates of return are the same? What we are witnessing here is the difference between the arithmetic and the geometric rates of return. One merely calculates an average. The other shows how the actual money in the account would have performed.

Of course as an investor the geometric return is the only one that concerns you. The difference is caused by volatility in the account and the geometric reality that it is harder to earn back money once you lose it.

To make it easier let me give another example. If you start with $100,000 and lost 50% you would have $50,000. If you then gained back that 50% you would still only have

$75,000. Between the two years you would have an arithmetic rate of return of Zero, yet your geometric rate would actually be a 25% loss.

Using this fuzzy math of investing, you can see how it is actually possible to average a 15% annual return, and lose money. I don't know about you but when my broker tells me he has an investment that averages 15%, I better not be losing money with it.

What all this says to the investor is that the more volatile an account is, the less real dollar return it will have, given the same rate of return. Let me say that again. The greater the volatility, the less money you will have in your account given the same average rate of return. This is why mutual funds publish what they call their Standard Deviation. Standard Deviation, or SD is the measurement of volatility in a fund. The greater the volatility the more you should be concerned about this fuzzy math eating away at your portfolio.

When you set up your account it is important that you consider how all the pieces of the puzzle work together. I know many investors who in the late 90's didn't want any bonds in their accounts because the stocks were doing so well. Wise ones recognized that bonds played an important role in stabilizing the account during market drops, and this reduction in volatility can have the effect of increasing real gains over time.

When you set up your account, rates of return are important, but do not overlook the portfolio as a whole. Strive to find investments that will complement each other and attempt to achieve your goals with as little total volatility, or deviation as possible.

Myth: 5% is 5%

Truth: There are several ways to calculate average returns. The only one that really matters is the one that puts more money in your pocket.

(examples given in this chapter are merely for illustrative purposes and do not represent any specific investment)

21 – Unbiased Advice

A frustrated investor made an appointment with me and right off the bat he declared with great emphasis, "All I want is some unbiased advice."

I paused for a moment then with a smile replied, "Well you're not going to get it here."

Let's be realistic. Humans are biased creatures. Our opinions and beliefs are formed from past experience. Our decisions are made based on numerous factors not the least of which is the #1 need to survive. When you walk into a brokers office, or an insurance office, or a doctors office or any office, you are dealing with someone who has set up that office to make money. They may be there to help you, they may have the greatest of intentions, but in the end their need to survive is still paramount in their mind

This doesn't mean that their decisions will not be in your best interests, because usually they will be, but it will also be in their interests too.

You cannot avoid bias in any decision, but if you are aware of the bias and where it comes from, it will assist you in sifting through it. Let me point out a few examples that are often overlooked.

1 - You broker with ABC Corp.. When your advisor gives you recommendations for investments, it seems that all of them are ABC investments. This doesn't mean they are not the right investments for you, but it should at least catch your attention that of the over 14,000 investments available, the ones that are perfect for you just happen to be the ones managed by the firm giving you the advice.

2 – You attend a seminar sponsored by an insurance agent who is not licensed to sell securities. When you meet with him in his office, it shouldn't surprise you to learn that he has an insurance answer for all your financial needs that usually includes an annuity.

3 – Your advisor works in a high-rise office in an expensive downtown location. All over his walls are pictures of him golfing with famous people at

exotic courses around the world. When you get your opinion from him it seems to be a little aggressive for your tastes, but he assures you that is what he does with all his best clients. It is possible that his "best" clients have very different financial goals than you do.

4 – You have finally found the perfect unbiased advice. You read an article in a major magazine by a brilliant former advisor who tells you that *you* don't need advisors at all; that you can do much better just by listening to his radio show. What you may not realize is that this person is not a former advisor at all. He is merely advising in a different format. He is trying to get you as a client. He makes his money writing articles, speaking on T.V. and radio, and convincing people to start listening to his advice. You see, even he cannot be totally unbiased because his ultimate goal is to get more people to listen to him and he does that by convincing them to stop listening to someone else.

It would appear I am telling you that no one can be trusted. Of course that is not true. As I have said before, my experience is that most advisors are honorable and only differ in their levels of understanding of the products and the clients. However, just as you should question the advice from your doctor, and often seek a second opinion; just as you would question the recommendation from your auto mechanic; just as you would think about the counsel given you by your neighbors, friends or religious leader, you should also give serious thought to advice from your financial professional. They are there to help you, but in the end, it is your money and you care about it more than anyone does.

Myth: It is possible to find unbiased advice on financial matters.

Truth: Not so long as humans remain human. And in reality, you wouldn't want unbiased advice. You want to know how you advisor really feels so you can make a good decision.

FINAL THOUGHTS

I was recently visiting Niagara Falls. What a powerful show of nature to see all that water in its power and majesty cascading over the edge to the valley below. Sights like this are both inspiring and humbling as we recognize how small we really are when compared to the wonder of the world around us.

While taking a tour of the falls, our guide pointed out how many people have gone over the Canadian Horseshoe falls in barrels and other contraptions designed to help the occupant survive the force of the falls and successfully cheat death. A young boy in our group raised his hand and asked, "Is it safe? Is it safe to go over the falls?" The guide thought for a minute then replied, "For half the people it was."

I start my days quite early because I need to catch up on all the world financial news. Sometimes I begin to feel like I am facing Niagara Falls. There is so much information, so many options, so many risks and rewards, and it just keeps coming. Like the little boy in our group I often find myself wondering if it is safe.

Safe is a relative word. Flying is safe, when compared to driving, but neither is as safe as the lounge chair on your porch. On the other hand, many an accident has happened on those loungers.

When going over the falls some feel safe in a wooden barrel, others need a more high-tech foam filled titanium tank to feel secure. Still more only feel safe if they are at home watching the whole thing on T.V.. Whatever your comfort level, there are plenty of options for everyone.

Investing is a risk most people are required to take. It has been wisely said that the risk of investing, whatever it may be, is less than the risk of doing nothing. The key is to go into it with as much information, or with as skilled a guide as possible.

While flying home from Atlanta one day our plane encountered more than the usual turbulence. So much so that one of the flight attendants was thrown into the laps of three gentlemen in the seats in front of me. At that point some passengers behind me began to scream and others were looking frantically around for comfort.

I turned and looked out my window and thought on the situation. The plane was bouncing around and it was hard to get your bearings due to the clouds outside the window. As is often the case with flying, there was a certain sense of helplessness.

As a pilot myself, I am no stranger to turbulence. I am not sure I fully understand what causes it, nor do I know what to do about it, but this I did know -- I knew that Boeing builds their planes to handle more turbulence than we were going through. I knew the pilots up front were well trained to fly in all kinds of weather. I knew the pilots had instruments at their disposal that could see, even though I couldn't, through the thickest of clouds.

And so I didn't worry. I didn't know what the next hours would bring in the way of comfort or lack thereof, but I was very confident that we would eventually land quite safely at our final destination; which we did.

Whether it be Niagara Falls, turbulent skies, or just a rough day in the market, there will often be times in life when we feel a little helpless; a little uneasy. Our investments will face rough times ahead and we may find ourselves losing sleep now and then.

Whenever I get in my airplane I understand the risks associated with flying miles above the earth in a man-made machine. I respect both the beauty and the hazards of flight. As such, I always gather as much information as possible about my plane, my course of travel, and the weather along the way. I am always ready to make course deviations if needed. I will even land and wait out extremely bad weather when warranted.

I place a high value on safety when flying, just as I place a high value on the benefits of it as well. I realize that if I stayed at home I would never risk injury in a plane accident. At the same time I would have missed out on a lifetime of the beautiful destinations flying has brought me.

There are no guarantees in investing, just as there are few guarantees in life in general. The key is to seek out an investment vehicle designed to weather the storms, get advice from someone who is well trained and current in their understandings, and be ever ready to make adjustments when the need arises. In so doing you will never fully eliminate risk, but you can keep it at a manageable level, and improve the likelihood of reaching your desired destination-which destination I have found to be well worth the effort.

THE BIG DISCLAIMER

Every book on financial matters must come with a big disclaimer, so here is mine. As of this writing I am licensed as a series 24 securities principal. That means in my office the buck and the blame stop with me. As such, it is important that you know the purpose of this book is not to give investment advice. If, after reading this book, you go out and make an investment decision without consulting a competent advisor, then don't blame me for the consequences. I do not know who you are. I do not know your situation, so I cannot give you advice. This book covers general financial topics and does so with stories from my own experiences. The stories are all true, though the names have been changed. The "myths" in this book are my own opinions. They are not designed to be taken as specific advice, nor do I guarantee any of my opinions are accurate or true-they are just mine. Take from this book what you can. Think about the topics and discuss them with your own financial advisor. Any reference to registered investment vehicles such as mutual funds etc., are used solely for the sake of discussion and not intended to be an offer or recommendation to buy or sell anything. In short – I am not giving you investment advice. I am merely trying to get you thinking. So read this book, think about it, speak to a CERTIFIED FINANCIAL PLANNER® and then make an informed decision.

Dan Wyson, CFP® received his formal education at UNLV and BYU. After receiving his bachelor's degree Dan went on to receive his designation as a CERTIFIED FINANCIAL PLANNER™.

Dan has written numerous articles relating to the financial industry for newspaper and magazine.

His common sense approach to financial planning, along with his sense of humor has made him a popular keynote speaker at countless business and non-profit functions throughout the western states.

He donates much of his time to mentor other financial professionals or to work with youth groups interested in learning about financial planning.

Dan and his talented wife Launa have 12wonderful children and are grandparents to an ever increasing number of lovely grandchildren. Their family is the focus of their life and you will find many of them working at the family firm - Wyson Financial.

"The 21 Financial Myths" is the result of literally thousands of client interviews, combined with many years of experience. By reading, it is hoped you may avoid some of the costly mistakes so many others have made.

Notes